WRITERS

ON ...

FOOD

AMELIA CARRUTHERS

CONTENTS

INTRODUCTION

Writing about carnal desires is a famously difficult task. Despite this, literature has had a long, intimate and controversial relationship with almost all our bodily needs. Since the advent of writing, food, drink and sex have served as consistent inspirations and plot devices. Both writers and readers have frequently argued however, that any reference to our more basic human needs will 'lower the tone' of an art-form traditionally thought to serve the higher ideals of our existence. Truth, love, beauty and tragedy are felt to be more fitting subjects. But to judge from the sheer amount of literary depictions of food, such sentiments miss their mark. Not only can depictions of food instigate desire, delight or disgust in the reader, but they also reveal just as much about the author, their culture and the literary character's inner workings. Food is, of course, everywhere, and is inextricably bound to our daily lives. Thus, it is only fitting that in moments of triumph and celebration, our cherished protagonists are blessed with opportunities to fulfil their instinctual drives. It is also equally telling, when, at times of change and doubt, the evocation of *food gone wrong* damns all involved. Writing on food, like writing on love, has the potential to convey both the highs and the lows of human existence.

Eating practices and conventions, the food chosen and one's company (or lack of it) are fundamental to fostering an understanding of society. But it is not so much the *rituals* that this book is concerned with, but the food itself. When food is portrayed, the reader is uncontrollably spirited into a shared experience with the diner, with only a few lines necessary to conjure up the quintessence of a dish. For instance, Mark Twain's extraordinary depiction of 'a mighty porterhouse steak an inch and a half thick, hot and sputtering from the griddle; dusted with fragrant pepper', or Emile Zola's 'strong-smelling cheeses', intense to the point of nausea, or even James Joyce's repellently evocative giblet soup; the 'nutty gizzards, a stuffed roast heart, liverslices fried with crustcrumbs, fried hencods' roes... which gave to his palate a fine tang of faintly scented urine.' Each of these passages elicits a visceral reaction; one can picture and taste the food being described – items to be salivated and savoured over. In this authentic, personal response, the reader is drawn deeper into the author's imaginative world.

Artistic depictions of food are nothing new, the most common themes in cave paintings are bison, cattle and deer. Still lifes traditionally adorned Minoan pots (around 1500 BC), and the wall-paintings of Pompeii are rife with images of fruit, vegetables and wine. In ancient Greek and Roman literature too, food played a central role not only in sustenance, but also in conversation and philosophising. The banquet gave rise to a specific genre, resulting in such classic works as Plato's *Symposium*, Xenophon's work of the same name, and the *Table Talk* of Plutarch's

Moralia. Roman comedies are notorious for their portrayals of seafood, complete with shopping lists, menus and recipes. Philemon's *Soldier* (a fourth century work) explains at length the guest's satisfaction over a baked river-fish, with the first man to 'discover the delights of the dish' leaping up and fleeing, 'taking the platter with him for a lap of the circuit, the others hot on his heels.' Such unfettered delight and abandon is rarely encountered elsewhere. Perhaps as a result of such behaviour, complex rules, sacraments and ceremonies involving food also appear in every major religious text. Even in our current age of plenty, food continues to inspire the literary and artistic mind.

'Food' is rife with contradictions. It is a corporal pleasure turned into the eternal sin of gluttony, as well as a vehicle for community, friendship and sharing that is, on a personal level, intractably individual. No one can ever experience the unique consciousness you feel when enjoying a fine soup, or a crusty piece of bread and butter. Even if Herman Melville's Ishmael had described every single ingredient in his fine clam chowder (and indeed, a whole chapter is given over to the endeavour), and we had learned everything about the physiology of taste, we would still be no closer to his own, unique impressions of the dish. But through the literary imagination, we can go some way to tasting for ourselves: the 'small juicy clams, scarcely bigger than hazel nuts, mixed with pounded ship biscuit, and salted pork cut up into little flakes; the whole enriched with butter, and plentifully seasoned with pepper and salt.' Within this incongruous world of tastes forever unknown yet perfectly understood, *Writers on… Food* summons up a world both starving and stuffed. The inherent juxtaposition is evident in the very beginnings of the word *Dining*. It comes from the thirteenth century French *disner,* 'to take the first meal of the day', which in turn stems from the Gallo-Romance *desjunare* 'to break one's fast.' *Dis* translates as 'undo' whilst *Jejunus* means 'fasting, or hungry.' Instantly, in the concept of the feast, the idea of famine is encompassed.

The transition from food as sustenance, to food as feast, to food as gastronomy; an art as well as a science, occurred relatively late. Whilst the English scholar and physician, Robert Burton stated in 1621 that 'Cookery is become an art, a noble science', the term 'gastronomy' only appeared in 1801. This was in a poem, by the French writer Joseph Berchoux, entitled *Gastronomie* – 'The laws that govern the stomach'. The most famous and influential *gourmand* was another Frenchman, Jean Anthelme Brillat-Savarin, who penned *The Physiology of Taste: Or, Meditations on Transcendental Gastronomy* (1825). According to Brillat-Savarin, 'Gastronomy is the knowledge and understanding of all that relates to man as he eats. Its purpose is to ensure the conservation of men, using the best food possible.' For a man who dedicated his whole life to the pleasures of the table, the key aspect of gastronomy was not 'the best food possible', this was the secondary clause, but primary was 'ensuring conversation of men.' And here lies the literary interest. For those to whom food and fine dining are readily available, it represents freedom and community, for those lacking this most fundamental of needs, it is an all consuming concern.

In Flaubert's *Madame Bovary,* the sheer scale of the wedding feast signals romantic yearnings and unfulfilled desires spiralling out of control – freedom gone horribly wrong. On the other hand, for Virginia Woolf, a perfectly tender 'Boeuf au Daube' is able to reconcile a troubled relationship, providing a brief respite from the dark and troubled world outside the home. Most potent of all, is when food is lacking. Charles Dickens's Oliver Twist, 'desperate with hunger, and reckless with misery' is lambasted and thrown out of his orphanage for having more of an appetite than the establishment deemed fitting. Because food imagery is a source of such deeply embedded associations, and because the innate sensuality of food engages not just the sense of taste, but of smell, touch, sight - and even hearing (sizzling, slurping and crunching), depictions of food evoke a mass of memories. Marcel Proust's *petites madeleines,* 'squat, plump little cakes' given to the narrator by his mother, are a paramount example of this involuntary rush of recollections. Even the humblest of works, for instance one of the earliest recorded nursery rhymes, 'Pat-a-cake, pat-a-cake, baker's man' signal a wealth of associations, far beyond the simple items described.

Writers on… Food demonstrates the ability of this most humble of subjects to enhance the reader's understanding of a text, its author, characters, the dish itself – and the wider world around us. This collection is intended as a comprehensive introduction, across time and geographical location, to the world's most influential writers, and their thoughts on *food*. As the following excerpts and quotations will demonstrate, our gustatory pleasures (and displeasures) are as varied as they are universal, as primordial as they are contemporary and as frivolous as they are necessary. They combine to form an irrational (if delicious!) jumble of comedy, calamities and fulfilment.

ON THE IMPORTANCE OF DINING...

To eat is a necessity, but to eat intelligently is an art.

– François La Rochefoucauld (1613-1680), *Réflexions ou Sentences et Maximes Morales* (1665); a collection of pithy, elegant observations, reflecting on the conduct of mankind. Of the 504 'maxims', the vast majority consist of just two or three lines.

My definition of man is a cooking animal. The beasts have memory, judgement, and the faculties and passions of our minds in a certain degree; but no beast is a cook.... Man alone can dress a good dish; and every man whatever is more or less a cook, in seasoning what he himself eats.

– James Boswell (1740-1795), *Journal of a Tour to the Hebrides with Samuel Johnson, LL.D* (1785). Journal entry made on Sunday 15th August, 1773.

An epicure, I mean to sing
    The table, as a subject fitting;
'T is certainly a useful thing,
    And friendship's ties is ever knitting.
Censure its weapons may unsheathe,
    To stop my song it is unable;
So, fearless of the critic's teeth,
    I here discourse upon the table.

A tribute must be due, of course,
    To such an universal mother.
Of life the table is the source;
    Indeed, my friend, I know no other.
The pillow, where you lay your head,
    Is soft, but raises visions sable:
The dying wretch is on his bed,
    The jolly dog is at his table.

A dish that scatters rich perfumes
    Must charm the sense beyond all
measure,–
The anxious nose the steam consumes,
    Inhaling mighty draughts of pleasure:
Compared to feasting, songs, and mirth,
    All other joys are but unstable;
The coldest heart that beats on earth
    Is melted by a smoking table.

Two rivals hear the church clock tell
    The moment that their life will take fast;
The second knows his business well,
    Who asks them both to come to breakfast.
All anger soon in wine is drowned,–
    To do such wonders wine is able,–
The rivals had been underground,
    Had they not rather sat at table.

Fat Raymond's door is every day
    Besieged by countless cabs and chaises,
City and court their visits pay,
    And all alike resound his praises.
'His virtues, then, must be most rare,
    That thus his fame mounts up like Babel.'
'Not so.' – 'Then vast his talents are?'
    'No; but he keeps a first-rate table.'

At table on affairs we muse,
    At table marriage contracts settle,
At table win, and sometimes lose,
    At table wrangling shows our mettle;
At table Cupid plumes his wing,
    At table we write truth or fable,
At table we do everything,
    So let us never leave the table.

– Marc-Antoine Madeleine Désaugiers (1772-1827); on the joys of the table. Désaugiers was
a French composer and dramatist, most of whose poetry was published in *Chansons et Poésies
Diverses,* which appeared in the same year as his death (1827).

Ponder well on this point: the pleasant hours of our life are all connected by a more or less tangible link, with some memory of the table.

– Charles Monselet (1825-1888), a French journalist, novelist, poet and playwright nicknamed 'the king of the gastronomes.'

We may live without poetry, music, and art;

We may live without conscience, and live without heart;

We may live without friends; we may live without books;

But civilized man cannot live without cooks.

He may live without books,—what is knowledge but grieving?

He may live without hope,—what is hope but deceiving?

He may live without love,—what is passion but pining?

But where is the man that can live without dining?

– Edward Robert Bulwer Lytton (1831-1891), *Lucile,* Part I, canto ii (1860). Lytton was
an English statesman and popular poet who served as Viceroy of India between 1876
and 1880.

What does 'cooking' mean? ... It means the knowledge of Medea, and of Circe, and of Calypso, and of Helen, and of Rebekah, and of the Queen of Sheba. It means the knowledge of all herbs, and fruits, and balms, and spices; and of all that is healing and sweet in fields and groves, and savoury in meats; it means carefulness, and inventiveness, and watchfulness, and willingness, and readiness of appliance; it means the economy of your great-grandmothers, and the science of modern chemists; it means much tasting, and no wasting; it means English thoroughness, and French art, and Arabian hospitality; and it means, in fine, that you are to be perfectly, and always, 'ladies' - 'loaf givers'.

– John Ruskin (1819-1900), the leading social critic of the Victorian era, giving a lecture to a girls' school in 1877. Within the lecture, Ruskin outlined the 'three feminine virtues' which he saw as: 'to be intensely happy' (to 'dance'), to dress beautifully (yourselves, 'your houses, and your gardens') and to cook.

I HATE PEOPLE WHO ARE NOT SERIOUS ABOUT MEALS. IT IS SO SHALLOW OF THEM.

– Oscar Wilde (1854-1900), *The Importance of Being Earnest, A Trivial Comedy for Serious People* (1895). Act I; Algernon speaking to Jack. First performed on 14th February 1895 at the St. James's Theatre in London, the play forms a withering attack on Victorian social conventions.

Part of the secret of a success in life is to eat what you like and let the food fight it out inside.

– Samuel Langhorne Clemens (1835-1910), better known by his *nom de plume* Mark Twain.

La bonne cuisine est la base du
véritable bonheur.

(Good food is the foundation of
genuine happiness.)

– Georges Auguste Escoffier (1846-1935), the legendary French chef, restaurateur and
culinary writer – one of the most important leaders in the development of modern
French cuisine.

The dinner was a somewhat formidable business. Dining with the van der Luydens was at best no light matter, and dining there with a Duke who was their cousin was almost a religious solemnity. It pleased Archer to think that only an old New Yorker could perceive the shade of difference (to New York) between being merely a Duke and being the van der Luydens' Duke. New York took stray noblemen calmly, and even (except in the Struthers set) with a certain distrustful hauteur; but when they presented such credentials as these they were received with an old-fashioned cordiality that they would have been greatly mistaken in ascribing solely to their standing

– Edith Wharton (1863-1937), *The Age of Innocence* (1920). In a book which mentions 'dinner' and 'dining' *sixty-nine* times, little mention is made of the food itself. Instead, Wharton utilises the complex rituals surrounding turn-of-the-century American dining to expose her characters and satirise the social elites of the day.

The human frame being what it is, heart, body and brain all mixed together, and not contained in separate compartments as they will be no doubt in another million years, a good dinner is of great importance to good talk. One cannot think well, love well, sleep well, if one has not dined well. The lamp in the spine does not light on beef and prunes.

– Virginia Woolf (1882-1941), *A Room of One's Own* (1929), a book-length essay which also contains the famous dictum, 'A woman must have money and a room of her own if she is to write fiction.'

ANTIQUITY: THE GREEKS & THE ROMANS

A crust eaten in peace is better than a banquet partaken in anxiety.

– Aesop (620-564 BCE), the Ancient Greek fabulist and author of *Aesop's Fables*.

If you pour oil and vinegar into the

same vessel, you would call them not

friends but opponents.

– Aeschylus (*c.* 525-456 BCE), the first of the three ancient Greek tragedians whose plays can still be read or performed (the others being Sophocles and Euripides). Clytaemestra speaking in *Agamemnon*, originally performed in 458 BCE.

LET FOOD BE THY MEDICINE AND MEDICINE BE THY FOOD.

– Hippocrates of Cos (460-370 BCE), an ancient Greek physician of the Age of Pericles, considered one of the most outstanding figures in medicinal history.

And what, Socrates, is the food of the soul? Surely, I said, knowledge is the food of the soul.

– Plato (*c.*428-348 BCE), *Protagoras*, or *The Sophists* (380 BCE), Hippocrates conversing with Socrates – primarily on whether or not 'virtue' can be taught.

I will unfold, or wherefore what to some
Is foul and bitter, yet the same to others
Can seem delectable to eat,- why here
So great the distance and the difference is
That what is food to one to some becomes
Fierce poison, as a certain snake there is
Which, touched by spittle of a man, will waste
And end itself by gnawing up its coil.
Again, fierce poison is the hellebore
To us, but puts the fat on goats and quails.

– Lucretius (99-55 BCE) was a Roman poet and philosopher. His only known work is the epic philosophical poem, *De Rerum Natura,* quoted above ('Book IV'). Here, Lucretius outlines the Epicurean maxim that what is one man's food may be another man's poison.

Nemini fidas, nisi cum quo prius multos modios salis absumpseris.

(Trust no one unless you have eaten much salt with him.)

– Marcus Tullius Cicero (106-43 BCE), the Roman philosopher, politician and orator. The above quotation is found in *Laelius De Amicitia* (a treatise on friendship written in 44 BCE), referring to the importance of keeping old friends.

The bulb preserved from th' plant in water doth
He rinse, and throw it into th' hollow stone.
On these he sprinkles grains of salt, and cheese
Is added, hard from taking up the salt.
Th' aforesaid herbs he now doth introduce
And with his left hand 'neath his hairy groin
Supports his garment;' with his right he first

The reeking garlic with the pestle breaks,
Then everything he equally doth rub
I' th' mingled juice. His hand in circles move:
Till by degrees they one by one do lose
Their proper powers, and out of many comes
A single colour, not entirely green
Because the milky fragments this forbid,
Nor showing white as from the milk because
That colour's altered by so many herbs.
The vapour keen doth oft assail the man's
Uncovered nostrils, and with face and nose
Retracted doth he curse his early meal;
With back of hand his weeping eyes he oft
Doth wipe, and raging, heaps reviling on
The undeserving smoke.

– Virgil (70-19 BCE), 'Moretum' which is usually translated from the Latin as 'Salad',
however the poem would be better described as 'Pesto'. In it, Virgil (at length) describes
how to make a cheese, garlic and herb paste.

It is certainly not lions and wolves that we eat out of self-defence; on the contrary, we ignore these and slaughter harmless, tame creatures without stings or teeth to harm us, creatures that, I swear, Nature appears to have produced for the sake of their beauty and grace. But nothing abashed us, not the flower-like tinting of the flesh, not the persuasiveness of the harmonious voice, not the cleanliness of their habits or the unusual intelligence that may be found in the poor wretches. No, for the sake of a little flesh we deprive them of sun, of light, of the duration of life to which they are entitled by birth and being.

– Plutarch (46-120 CE), outlining a basis for vegetarianism. Plutarch was a Greek (and later Roman) historian, biographer and essayist, known primarily for his *Parallel Lives* and the *Moralia*.

How good it is, when you have roast meat or suchlike foods before you, to impress on your mind that this is the dead body of fish, this the dead body of a bird or a pig; and again, that the Falernian wine is the mere juice of grapes... How good these perceptions are at getting to the heart of the real thing and penetrating through it, so you can see it for what it is!

– Marcus Aurelius (121-180 CE), the last of the Five Good Emperors and one of the most important Roman stoic philosophers. The quote above comes from his *Meditations;* a series of personal reflections setting forth his ideas on Stoic Philosophy.

For a yearning stole up on me to go forth and tell the world, and not only the world but the heavens too, how I prepared the dish - By Athena, how sweet it is to get it right every time - What a fish it was I had tender before me! What a dish I made of it! Not drugged senseless with cheeses, nor window-boxed with dandifying herbs, it emerged from the oven as naked as the day it was born. So tender, so soft was the fire I invested in the cooking of it. You wouldn't believe the result. It was just like when a chicken gets hold of something bigger than she can swallow and runs around in a circle, unable to let it out of her sight, determined to get it down, while the other chickens chase after her. It was just the same: the first man among them to discover the delights of the dish leapt up and fled taking the platter with him for a lap of the circuit, the others hot on his heels. I allowed myself a shriek of joy, as some snatched at something, some snatched at everything and others snatched at nothing at all. And yet I had merely taken into my care some mud-eating river fish. If I had got hold of something more exceptional, a 'little grey' from Attica, say, or a boar-fish from [Amphilochian] Argos, or from dear old Sicyon the fish that Poseidon carries to the gods in heaven, a conger-eel, then everyone would have attained to a state of divinity. I have discovered the secret of eternal life; men already dead I make to walk again, once they but smell it in their nostrils.

– Philemon's *Soldier* (a fourth century comedy). Amusingly enough there are myriad references in fourth-century comedies to the consumption of fish; shopping lists for fish, fish menus and fish dishes – the above being just one example.

THE RENAISSANCE

L'anima mia gustava di quel cibo,
Che saziando di sè, di sè s'asseta.

(My soul tasted that heavenly food,
Which gives new appetite while
it satiates.)

– Dante Alighieri (*c.* 1265-1321), *Purgatorio,* XXXI; the second part of Dante's *Divine Comedy,* following the *Inferno,* and preceding the *Paradiso.* The poem was written in the early 14th century.

I AM FED WITH THAT FOOD WHICH IS MINE ALONE.

– Niccolò Machiavelli (1469-1527), the author of *The Prince,* in a letter to Francesco Vettori on 13th December 1513. Machiavelli was dismissed from office (and subsequently tortured) by the Medici family in 1512. He is here describing his life during self-exile at his country estate at San Casciano.

Bread is not our only food: and that without toyling our common mother nature hath with great plentie stored us with whatsoever should be needfull for us, yea, as it is most likely, more richly and amply than now adaies she doth, that we have added so much art unto it. The gluttonous excesse and intemperate lavishnesse of our appetite exceeding all the inventions we endevour to finde out wherewith to glut and cloy the same.

– Michel de Montaigne (1533-1592), Chapter XII 'An Apologie of Raymond Sabond', the longest of the *Essais* (1580); an extended expression of Montaigne's philosophical skepticism.

Capulet: So many guests invite as here are writ.

(to second servingman) Sirrah, go hire me twenty cunning cooks.

Second Servingman: You shall have none ill, sir, for I'll try if they can lick their fingers.

Capulet: How canst thou try them so?

Second Servingman: Marry, sir, 'tis an ill cook that cannot lick his own fingers. Therefore he that cannot lick his fingers goes not with me.

Capulet: Go, be gone.

– William Shakespeare (1564-1616), Capulet planning the wedding party; Act 4, scene 4, of *Romeo and Juliet* (*c*. 1591).

If music be the food of love, play on;

Give me excess of it, that, surfeiting,

The appetite may sicken, and so die.

– William Shakespeare (1564-1616), the Duke Orsino speaking in Act 1, scene 1 of
Twelfth Night (1602).

Do you think because you are virtuous, that there shall be no more cakes and ale?

– William Shakespeare (1564-1616), Act 2, scene 3: Olivia's House, in *Twelfth Night*. Sir Toby Belch speaking to the Clown.

Some books are to be tasted, others are to be

swallowed, and some few to be chewed and digested.

– Francis Bacon (1561-1626), the English philosopher, statesman and essayist. Labelled
the father of empiricism and progenitor of the *Baconian method* or simply, the
Scientific Method.

Dapple was lying on his back, and Sancho helped him to his feet, which he was scarcely able to keep; and then taking a piece of bread out of his alforjas which had shared their fortunes in the fall, he gave it to the ass, to whom it was not unwelcome, saying to him as if he understood him, *'With bread all sorrows are less'*.

– Miguel de Cervantes Saavedra (1547-1616); a Spanish novelist, poet and playwright, best known for his magnum opus, *Don Quixote* (1605-1615), considered to be the first modern European novel.

Cookery is become an art, a noble science; cooks are gentlemen.

– Robert Burton (1577-1640), an English scholar at Oxford University, best known for *The Anatomy of Melancholy* (1621), from where this quotation comes; Part I, Section II.

For pottage and puddings
and custards and pies,

Our pumpkins and parsnips
are common supplies,

We have pumpkins at morning
and pumpkins at noon,

If it were not for pumpkins
we should be undoon.

– American Pilgrim Verse, circa 1630. Pumpkins were an incredibly important food source for the early American pilgrims, as they stored well (which meant food during winter). They were reportedly served at the second Thanksgiving celebration.

Would ye have fresh cheese and cream?

Julia's breast can give you them:

And, if more, each nipple cries:

To your cream here's strawberries.

– Robert Herrick (1591-1674), 'Fresh Cheese and Cream' (published in *Hesperides* in
1648). Herrick was an English poet and cleric – the fourth son of Julia Stone.

The hungry man takes no thought for his meat,

Though his stomach would brook a ten-penny nail;

He quite forgets hunger, thinks on it no longer,

If he touch but the sparks of a pot of good ale.

The poor man will praise it so hath he good cause,

That all the year eats neither partridge nor quail,

But sets up his rest and makes up his feast,

With a crust of brown bread and a pot of good ale.

– Old English Song, from *An Antidote Against Melancholy: Made up in Pills. Compounded of witty ballads, jovial songs, and merry catches* (published in 1661).

Govern well thy appetite, lest Sin

Surprise thee, and her black attendant Death.

– John Milton (1608-1674), *Paradise Lost* (1667), Book VII. An epic poem in blank verse, considered by critics to be Milton's greatest work. It helped solidify his reputation as one of the foremost English poets of his time.

You and people like you, that a table overloaded with eatables is a real cut-throat; that, to be the true friends of those we invite, frugality should reign throughout the repast we give, and that according to the saying of one of the ancients, *'We must eat to live, and not live to eat.'*

– Molière (1622-1673), The Miser, ('L'Avare'), Act 5, scene 3. A five-act prose comedy, first performed on 9th September 1668 in the theatre of the Palais-Royal in Paris. Valerie speaking to Harpagon.

COOLNESS OF THE MELONS

FLECKED WITH MUD

IN THE MORNING DEW.

– Matsuo Bash (1644-1694), the most famous poet of the Edo period in Japan. He is recognised as the greatest master of haiku (then called hokku), and in this simple verse 'Coolness of the Melons' depicts the wonders of these fresh fruits.

Pat-a-cake, pat-a-cake, baker's man,
Bake me a cake as fast as you can;
Pat it and prick it and mark it with B,
Put it in the oven for baby and me.

Patty cake, patty cake, baker's man.
Bake me a cake as fast as you can;
Roll it up, roll it up;
And throw it in a pan!
Patty cake, patty cake, baker's man.

– One of the oldest surviving English nursery rhymes. The earliest recorded version appears in Thomas D'Urfey's play *The Campaigners* from 1698, where a nurse says to her charges: '...and pat a cake Bakers man, so I will master as I can, and prick it, and prick it, and prick it, and prick it, and prick it, and throw't into the Oven.'

THE LONG
NINETEENTH
CENTURY

FOOLS MAKE FEASTS AND WISE MEN EAT THEM.

– Benjamin Franklin (1706-1790), one of the Founding Fathers of the Unites States and in many ways 'the First American.'

When mighty Roast Beef was the Englishman's food,
It ennobled our brains and enriched our blood.
Our soldiers were brave and our courtiers were good
Oh! the Roast Beef of old England,
And old English Roast Beef!
But since we have learnt from all-vapouring France
To eat their ragouts as well as to dance,
We're fed up with nothing but vain complaisance
Oh! the Roast Beef of Old England,
And old English Roast Beef!
Our fathers of old were robust, stout, and strong,
And kept open house, with good cheer all day long,
Which made their plump tenants rejoice in this song–
Oh! The Roast Beef of old England,
And old English Roast Beef!

– Henry Fielding (1707-1754), 'The Roast Beef of Old England', a patriotic ballad written for *The Grub-Street Opera* (first performed in 1731). The tune was so popular it was given a new setting by the composer Richard Leveridge, and became the customary song for theatre audiences to sing before, after, and occasionally during, any new play. The Royal Navy still play the tune before going in to dine at Mess Dinners.

A woman should never be seen eating or drinking, unless it be lobster salad and Champagne, the only true feminine and becoming viands.

– Lord Byron (1788-1824), writing to Lady Melbourne on 25th September 1812. He describes a beautiful Italian lady with dark eyes who will save him the 'trouble of marrying.' Her only fault, in Byron's eyes, was that she ate too much.

Man is a carnivorous production,

And must have meals, at least one meal a day;

He cannot live, like woodcocks, upon suction,

But, like the shark and tiger, must have prey;

Although his anatomical construction

Bears vegetables, in a grumbling way,

Your labouring people think beyond all question,

Beef, veal, and mutton better for digestion.

– Lord Byron (1788-1824), *Don Juan,* Canto II. When the first two cantos were published anonymously in 1819, the poem was criticised for its 'immoral content' though it was also an immediate popular success.

Though we eat little flesh and drink no wine,

Yet let's be merry; we'll have tea and toast;

Custards for supper, and an endless host

Of syllabubs and jellies and mincepies,

And other such ladylike luxuries, —

Feasting on which we will philosophize!

– Percy Bysshe Shelley (1792-1822), one of the major English Romantic poets; a radical in his poetry as well as his political and social views. 'Letter to Maria Gisborne' (1st July 1820), from *Posthumous Poems* (1824).

The discovery of a new dish does more for the happiness of the human race than the discovery of a star.

A meal without cheese is like a beautiful woman who lacks an eye.

He who receives friends and pays no attention to the repast prepared for them, is not fit to have friends.

– Jean Anthelme Brillat-Savarin (1755-1826), 'Aphorisms of the professor' from *The Physiology of Taste: Or, Meditations on Transcendental Gastronomy* (1825). The book has never been out of print since it first appeared; a timeless discussion on the pleasures of the table.

There, on a slope of orchard, Francis laid
A damask napkin wrought with horse and hound,
Brought out a dusky loaf that smelt of home,
And, half-cut-down, a pasty costly-made,
Where quail and pigeon, lark and leveret lay,
Like fossils of the rock, with golden yolks
Imbedded and injellied; last, with these,
A flask of cider from his father's vats,
Prime, which I knew; and so we sat and ate
And talked old matters over...

– Alfred Lord Tennyson (1809-1892), 'Audley Court' (1838), written during an excursion
to Torquay. Tennyson was Poet Laureate of Great Britain and Ireland during much of
Queen Victoria's reign, and remains one of the country's most popular bards.

No one was irritable; we have never known anyone to remain unhappy while digesting a good meal. We enjoy lingering in a becalmed state, a kind of midpoint between the reverie of a thinker and the contentment of a cud-chewing animal, a state that should be termed the physical melancholy of gastronomy.

– Honoré de Balzac (1799-1850), a French novelist and playwright best known for his *La Comédie Humaine* (1842), which presents a panorama of French life in the years after the 1815 fall of Napoleon Bonaparte.

The greatest delight the fields and woods minister is the suggestion of an occult relation between man and the vegetable. I am not alone and unacknowledged. They nod to me and I to them.

– Ralph Waldo Emerson (1803-1882), *Nature* (1836). Emerson was one of the great American naturalists, and a champion of the transcendentalist movement.

ANY HEALTHY MAN CAN GO WITHOUT FOOD FOR TWO DAYS - BUT NOT WITHOUT POETRY.

– Charles Baudelaire (1821-1867), the French poet famous for *Les Fleurs du Mal* (1857), a work which expresses the changing nature of beauty in modern, industrializing Paris.

'When the parlour fire gets low, put coals on the ketchen fire!'... Such is man! no use in havin' their hearts if ye don't have their stomachs.

...Only mind me and mark me: don't neglect your cookery. Kissing don't last: cookery do!

– George Meredith (1828-1909), an English novelist and poet of the Victorian era. Mrs Berry providing some 'matrimonial wisdom' to Lucy in 'Chapter XXVIII' from *The Ordeal of Richard Feverel* (1859).

They dined on mince, and slices of quince,
    Which they ate with a runcible spoon;
And hand in hand, on the edge of the sand,
    They danced by the light of the moon,
        The moon,
        The moon,
They danced by the light of the moon.

– Edward Lear (1812-1888), 'The Owl and the Pussycat', first published in 1871 as part of *Nonsense Songs, Stories, Botany and Alphabets*. Lear was an English artist, author and poet, known chiefly for his use of literary nonsense in poetry and prose. The word 'runcible' was apparently one of Lear's favourite inventions, appearing in several of his works.

Man lives not by bread alone. But dost Thou know that for the sake of that earthly bread the spirit of the earth will rise up against Thee... Dost Thou know that the ages will pass, and humanity will proclaim by the lips of their sages that there is no crime, and therefore no sin; there is only hunger?... Oh, never, never can they feed themselves without us! No science will give them bread so long as they remain free. In the end they will lay their freedom at our feet, and say to us, 'Make us your slaves, but feed us.' They will understand themselves, at last, that freedom and bread enough for all are inconceivable together, for never, never will they be able to share between them!

– Fyodor Dostoyevsky (1821-1881). 'Chapter V: The Grand Inquisitor' from *The Brothers Karamazov* (1880); Dostoyevsky's last philosophical and spiritual masterpiece.

Fame is a fickle food

Upon a shifting plate

Whose table once a

Guest but not

The second time is set.

Whose crumbs the crows inspect

And with ironic caw

Flap past it to the Farmer's Corn –

Men eat of it and die.

– Emily Dickinson (1830-1886), 'Fame is a Fickle Food' (published posthumously in 1924). Dickinson lived in almost total isolation, yet is now considered (alongside Walt Whitman) as the founder of a uniquely American poetic voice.

Man is the only animal that can remain on friendly terms with the victims he intends to eat until he eats them.

– Samuel Butler (1835-1902), an iconoclastic Victorian author famed for the utopian satire *Erewhon* (1872) and the semi-autobiographical novel, *The Way of All Flesh* (1903).

Appetite, n.: An instinct thoughtfully implanted by Providence as a solution to the labour question.

Bacon, n.: The mummy of a pig embalmed in 'save one's bacon' is to narrowly escape some particular woman or other peril.

Custard, n.: A detestable substance produced by a malevolent conspiracy of the hen, the cow, and the cook.

Deliberation, n.: The act of examining one's bread to determine which side it is buttered on.

Edible, adj.: Good to eat, and wholesome to digest, as a worm to a toad, a toad to a snake, a snake to a pig, a pig to a man, and a man to a worm.

– Ambrose Bierce (1842-1914), *The Devil's Dictionary* (1911). Bierce was an American editorialist, journalist and short story writer, most famed for his satirical lexicon, *The Devil's Dictionary*. His motto 'nothing matters' alongside his sardonic view of human nature and the wider world earned him the nickname 'Bitter Bierce.'

I did not wait to hear the end of my father's story, for

I had been with him myself after mass when we had met

M. Legrandin; instead, I went downstairs to the kitchen

to ask about the menu for our dinner, which was of fresh

interest to me daily, like the news in a paper, and excited

me as might the programme of a coming festivity.

– Marcel Proust (1871-1922), considered to be one of the greatest authors of all time.
Volume One, 'Swann's Way' of *À la Recherche du Temps Perdu* (1871-1922).

FOOD
AND FAITH

The true person governs by emptying the heart
of desire and filling the belly with food, weakening
ambitions and strengthening bones.

– Lao-Tzu (usually dated to around the sixth century BCE), was a philosopher and a
poet of ancient China, best known as the reputed author of the *Tao Te Ching* and the
founder of philosophical Taoism. Lao-Tzu is also revered as a deity in religious Taoism
and many traditional Chinese religions, which emphasise living in harmony with the
Tao (meaning 'path' or 'principle' – something that is both the source and driving force
behind everything that exists).

As evening approached, the disciples came to him and said, 'This is a remote place, and it's already getting late. Send the crowds away, so they can go to the villages and buy themselves some food.'

Jesus replied, 'They do not need to go away. You give them something to eat.'

'We have here only five loaves of bread and two fish,' they answered.

'Bring them here to me,' he said. And he directed the people to sit down on the grass. Taking the five loaves and the two fish and looking up to heaven, he gave thanks and broke the loaves. Then he gave them to the disciples, and the disciples gave them to the people. They all ate and were satisfied, and the disciples picked up twelve basketfuls of broken pieces that were left over. The number of those who ate was about five thousand men, besides women and children.

       – *The Bible,* (Mathew 12: 13-21), Jesus Feeding of the Five Thousand.

The eating of meat extinguishes the seed of great compassion.

– Guatama Buddha in The *Mahayana Mahaparinirvana Sutra;* one of the Tathgatagarbha stras of Mahyna Buddhism which originated in the first century CE in southern India.

O ye who believe! Eat of the good things wherewith We have provided you, and render thanks to Allah if it is (indeed) He whom ye worship.

– *The Qur'an* (Al-Baqra, Pickthal, 2:172). In the Qur'an, believers only have the right to eat animals because Allah has *given* the privilege.

The True food is the Lord's love. So says the True Guru. With the True food I am appeased and with Truth I am delighted.

– Guru Angad (1504-1552), the second of the ten Sikh Gurus and contributor to the Guru Granth Sahib, a voluminous text of 1430 *Angs* (pages), compiled and composed during the period of Sikh gurus, from 1469 to 1708.

The spirit cannot endure the body when overfed, but, if underfed, the body cannot endure the spirit.

– Francis de Sales (1567-1622), the Bishop of Geneva honoured as a Saint in the Roman Catholic Church. He became noted for his deep faith and gentle approach to the religious divisions in his land resulting from the Protestant Reformation.

Nothing would be more tiresome than eating and drinking if God had not made them a pleasure as well as a necessity.

– François-Marie Arouet, better known by his nom de plume: Voltaire (1694-1778).

Some hae meat and canna eat,

And some wad eat that want it,

But we hae meat and we can eat,

And sae the Lord be thankit.

– 'The Selkirk Grace', a prayer said afore eatin that's attreebute tae Robert Burns (1759-1796). In connection with the poet's visit to the seat of the Earl of Selkirk, Burns was asked to say Grace and reportedly delivered the lines above.

When you rise in the morning, give thanks for the light, for your life, for your strength. Give thanks for your food and for the joy of living. If you see no reason to give thanks, the fault lies in yourself.

– Tecumseh (1768-1813), a Native American leader of the Shawnee (a semi-migratory Native American nation) as well as a large tribal confederacy which opposed the United States during Tecumseh's War (1811).

There are people in the world so hungry, that God cannot appear to them except in the form of bread.

– Mahatma Gandhi (1869-1948); the pre-eminent leader of Indian nationalism in British ruled India, who inspired movements for civil rights and freedom across the world. Ghandi's vision was for a free India based on religious pluralism, and his non-violent civil disobedience was largely inspired by the Hindu teachings of love and equality.

Mayonnaise:

One of the sauces which

serve the French in place of

a state religion.

– Ambrose Bierce (1842-1914), *The Devil's Dictionary* (1911).

'They had some excuse,' said Clovis. 'They did it to save their immortal souls, didn't they? You needn't tell me that a man who doesn't love oysters and asparagus and good wines has got a soul, or a stomach either. He's simply got the instinct for being unhappy highly developed.'

Clovis relapsed for a few golden moments into tender intimacies with a succession of rapidly disappearing oysters.

'I think oysters are more beautiful than any religion,' he resumed presently. 'They not only forgive our unkindness to them; they justify it, they incite us to go on being perfectly horrid to them. Once they arrive at the supper-table they seem to enter thoroughly into the spirit of the thing. There's nothing in Christianity or Buddhism that quite matches the sympathetic unselfishness of an oyster.'

– Hector Hugh Munro (1870-1916), better known by the pen name 'Saki', a British writer whose witty, mischievous and sometimes macabre stories satirized Edwardian society and culture. 'The Match-Maker' from *The Chronicles of Clovis* (1911).

Man in his hunger for faith will feed his mind with
the nearest and most convenient food.

– F. Scott Fitzgerald (1896-1940), whose works are the paradigmatic writings of the Jazz
Age. The quotation above comes from *This Side of Paradise,* Fitzgerald's debut novel,
published in 1920.

BREAKFAST
VS. DINNER

Tonight, grave sir, both my poor house, and I
Do equally desire your company;
Not that we think us worthy such a guest,
But that your worth will dignify our feast
With those that come, whose grace may make that seem
Something, which else could hope for no esteem.
It is the fair acceptance, sir, creates
The entertainment perfect, not the cates.
Yet shall you have, to rectify your palate,
An olive, capers, or some better salad
Ushering the mutton; with a short-legged hen,
If we can get her, full of eggs, and then
Lemons, and wine for sauce; to these a cony
Is not to be despaired of, for our money;
And, though fowl now be scarce, yet there are clerks,
The sky not falling, think we may have larks.
I'll tell you of more, and lie, so you will come:
Of partridge, pheasant, woodcock, of which some
May yet be there, and godwit, if we can;
Knat, rail, and ruff too. Howsoe'er, my man
Shall read a piece of Virgil, Tacitus,

Livy, or of some better book to us,
Of which we'll speak our minds, amidst our meat;
And I'll profess no verses to repeat.
To this, if ought appear which I not know of,
That will the pastry, not my paper, show of.
Digestive cheese and fruit there sure will be;
But that which most doth take my Muse and me,
Is a pure cup of rich Canary wine,
Which is the Mermaid's now, but shall be mine;
Of which had Horace, or Anacreon tasted,
Their lives, as so their lines, till now had lasted.
Tobacco, nectar, or the Thespian spring,
Are all but Luther's beer to this I sing.
Of this we will sup free, but moderately,
And we will have no Pooley, or Parrot by,
Nor shall our cups make any guilty men;
But, at our parting we will be as when
We innocently met. No simple word
That shall be uttered at our mirthful board,
Shall make us sad next morning or affright
The liberty that we'll enjoy tonight.

– Ben Jonson (1572-1637), the famed English playwright, poet and literary critic, best
known for his satirical plays. 'Poem No. 101' of *The Epigrams* (1616): 'Inviting a Friend
to Supper' – on the wonders of fine dinners, honest food and civilised discourse.

...Strange to see how a good dinner and feasting reconciles everybody.

– Samuel Pepys (1633-1703), *The Diary of Samuel Pepys*, entry on Thursday 9th November 1665. Pepy's detailed private diary is one of the most important primary sources for the English Restoration period, combining personal reflections and eyewitness accounts of events such as the Plague epidemic and the Great Fire of London.

Lord Henry and his lady were the hosts;
The party we have touch'd on were the guests:
Their table was a board to tempt even ghosts
To pass the Styx for more substantial feasts.
I will not dwell upon ragouts or roasts,
Albeit all human history attests
That happiness for man—the hungry sinner!—
Since Eve ate apples, much depends on dinner.

– Lord Byron (1788-1824), 'Dinner: Thirteenth Canto' from *Don Juan* (1824), the satirical
poem based on the legend of Don Juan. Modern critics generally consider it Byron's
masterpiece, with a total of more than 16,000 lines of verse.

Alice laughed. 'There's no use trying,' she said. 'One can't believe impossible things.'

'I daresay you haven't had much practice,' said the Queen. 'When I was your age, I always did it for half-an-hour a day. Why, sometimes I've believed as many as six impossible things before breakfast. There goes the shawl again!'

– Charles Lutwidge Dodgson (1832-1898), better known as Lewis Carroll, author of *Through the Looking Glass and What Alice Found There* (1871). The Queen demonstrates just what can be accomplished before one's breakfast.

THERE IS ONLY ONE
DIFFERENCE BETWEEN A LONG
LIFE AND A GOOD DINNER:
THAT, IN THE DINNER, THE
SWEETS COME LAST.

– Robert Louis Stevenson (1850-1894), 'Will O' The Mill', Chapter III: 'Death' from
The Body Snatcher, The Suicide Club and Other Tales (first published in *Cornhill
Magazine*, 1878).

'Her cuisine is a little limited but she has as good an idea

of breakfast as a Scotchwoman. What have you here Watson?'

'Ham and eggs,' I answered. 'Good! What are you going to take,

Mr. Phelps – curried fowl or eggs, or will you help yourself?'

– Arthur Conan Doyle (1859-1930), *The Adventure of the Naval Treaty* (1893); Sherlock
Holmes speaking of Mrs Hudson's cooking. *The Naval Treaty* is one of fifty-six
Sherlock Holmes short stories, and one of the twelve stories collected in *The Memoirs of
Sherlock Holmes.*

You can't possibly ask me to go without having some dinner. It's absurd. I never go without my dinner. No one ever does, except vegetarians and people like that.

– Oscar Wilde (1854-1900), *The Importance of Being Earnest* (1895), Act II, Algernon speaking to Jack.

Who can begin conventional amiability the first thing in the morning? It is the hour of savage instincts and natural tendencies; it is the triumph of the Disagreeable and the Cross. I am convinced that the Muses and the Graces never thought of having breakfast anywhere but in bed.

– Elizabeth von Arnim (1866-1941), an Australian-born British novelist, who became Gräfin (Countess) von Arnim-Schlagenthin on her second marriage. The quotation above comes from *Elizabeth and Her German Garden* (1898); Arnim's first novel, a semi-autobiographical, brooding, yet satirical text.

There'll never be a perfect breakfast eaten until some man grows arms long enough to stretch down to New Orleans for his coffee & over to Norfolk for his rolls, & reaches up to Vermont & digs a slice of butter out of a spring-house, & then turns over a beehive close to a white clover patch out in Indiana for the rest. Then he'd come pretty close to making a meal on the amber that the gods eat on Mount Olympia.

– William Sydney Porter (1862-1910), better known as O. Henry; an American writer known for his wit, wordplay and warm characterization. *Hostages to Momus*, in which this quotation appears, was a short story inspired by the kidnapping of Ion Perdicaris in 1904.

'Couldn't you ask him here to dinner or something?' said the Mole.

'He wouldn't come,' replied the Rat simply. 'Badger hates Society, and invitations, and dinner, and all that sort of thing.'

– Kenneth Grahame (1859-1932), *The Wind in the Willows*, 'Chapter III: The Wild Wood' (1908) – a true of the classic of children's literature.

All around, on chairs and footstools, on and under the tables, even on the ground in a corner, the unwashed breakfast dishes of the tenants stood piled up. There were little cans where you could find a little coffee or milk, on many tiny plates were still some leftover butter, some bread rolls had tumbled far away from a large, fallen baking sheet. There was quite possibly a breakfast in everything taken together, which Brunelda wouldn't be able to put down if she never learned of its origins. As Karl thought about that and a glance at the clock showed him that they had already been waiting there a half hour and Brunelda was probably raging and Delamarche probably riled up against the servants, the woman yelled at them as she coughed – during which Karl stared at her – 'You can sit here, but the breakfast won't come. Come back in two hours for supper.'

'Come on, Robinson,' Karl said, 'we'll put the breakfast together ourselves.' 'How?' yelled the woman with an inclined head. 'Please be reasonable,' said Karl, 'why wouldn't you give us breakfast? We've been waiting now for half an hour already, that's long enough. You're paid for everything and we certainly pay a better price than all the others. Of course it's annoying for you that we breakfast so late, but we are your tenants, we have the habit of breakfasting late and you have to accommodate us a little. Today it's especially difficult because of your daughter's illness, but because of that we're prepared to put our breakfast together from the leftovers, so long as there's nothing else and you won't give us a fresh meal.'

– Franz Kafka (1883-1924), *Amerika: The Man Who Disappeared* (1911-1914); the incomplete first novel of Kafka, published posthumously in 1927. Here, Karl and Delmarche attempt to source Brunelda's breakfast.

My wife and I tried to breakfast together, but we had to stop or our marriage would have been wrecked... Breakfast should be had in bed, alone. Not downstairs, after one has dressed.

– Winston Churchill (1874-1965), the Prime Minister of the United Kingdom from 1940 to 1945 and again from 1951 to 1955, speaking to a friend.

APATHY
VS. APPETITE

Necessity demands our daily bread;

Hunger is insolent, and will be fed.

– Homer (8th century BCE), the author of the *Iliad* and the *Odyssey*, revered as the
greatest of the Greek epic poets.

MY APPETITE COMES TO ME WHILE EATING, AND NOT ELSE; I AM NEVER HUNGRY BUT AT TABLE.

– Michel de Montaigne (1533-1592), *Essais,* 'Chapter XVII; Of Vanity' (published 1580). Montaigne was one of the most important writers of the French Renaissance, chiefly known for popularising the 'essay' as a literary genre. To this day, they remain some of the most influential essays ever written.

....It happened one day that Little Two-eyes had to go out into the fields to take care of the goat, but she was still quite hungry because her sisters had given her so little to eat. So she sat down in the meadow and began to cry, and she cried so much that two little brooks ran out of her eyes. But when she looked up once in her grief there stood a woman beside her who asked, 'Little Two-eyes, what are you crying for?' Little Two-eyes answered, 'Have I not reason to cry? Because I have two eyes like other people, my sisters and my mother cannot bear me; they push me out of one corner into another, and give me nothing to eat except what they leave. To-day they have given me so little that I am still quite hungry.' Then the wise woman said, 'Little Two-eyes, dry your eyes, and I will tell you something so that you need never be hungry again. Only say to your goat,

'Little goat, bleat,
Little table, appear,'

and a beautifully spread table will stand before you, with the most delicious food on it, so that you can eat as much as you want. And when you have had enough and don't want the little table any more, you have only to say,

'Little goat, bleat,
Little table, away,'

and then it will vanish.' Then the wise woman went away.

But Little Two-eyes thought, 'I must try at once if what she has told me is true, for I am more hungry than ever'; and she said,

'Little goat, bleat,
Little table appear,'

and scarcely had she uttered the words, when there stood a little table before her covered with a white cloth, on which were arranged a plate, with a knife and fork and a silver spoon, and the most beautiful dishes, which were smoking hot, as if they had just come out of the kitchen. Then Little Two-eyes said the shortest grace she knew, and set to work and made a good dinner. And when she had had enough, she said, as the wise woman had told her,

'Little goat, bleat,
Little table, away,'

and immediately the table and all that was on it disappeared again. 'That is a splendid way of housekeeping,' thought Little Two-eyes, and she was quite happy and contented.

– *One-Eye, Two Eyes, and Three-Eyes,* a traditional German fairy tale first collected by the Brothers Grimm in *Children's and Household Tales* (1812). It was first printed in English (the translation above) by Andrew Lang in *The Green Fairy Book* (1892).

AN ARMY MARCHES ON ITS STOMACH.

– Napoleon Bonaparte (1769-1821), the *Emperor of the French* (from 1804-1814) who understood the importance of food. Widely regarded as one of the greatest commanders in history, his campaigns are still studied at military academies worldwide.

The evening arrived; the boys took their places. The master, in his cook's uniform, stationed himself at the copper; his pauper assistants ranged themselves behind him; the gruel was served out; and a long grace was said over the short commons. The gruel disappeared; the boys whispered each other, and winked at Oliver; while his next neighbours nudged him. Child as he was, he was desperate with hunger, and reckless with misery. He rose from the table; and advancing to the master, basin and spoon in hand, said: somewhat alarmed at his own temerity:

'Please, sir, I want some more.'

The master was a fat, healthy man; but he turned very pale. He gazed in stupefied astonishment on the small rebel for some seconds, and then clung for support to the copper. The assistants were paralysed with wonder; the boys with fear.

'What!' said the master at length, in a faint voice.

'Please, sir,' replied Oliver, 'I want some more.'

The master aimed a blow at Oliver's head with the ladle; pinioned him in his arm; and shrieked aloud for the beadle.

The board were sitting in solemn conclave, when Mr. Bumble rushed into the room in great excitement, and addressing the gentleman in the high chair, said,

'Mr. Limbkins, I beg your pardon, sir! Oliver Twist has asked for more!'

– Charles Dickens (1812-1870), *Oliver Twist, The Parish Boys Progress,* Chapter II (1838); the first Victorian novel with a child protagonist, responsible for exposing the cruel treatment of orphans in Victorian London.

His high spiced wares were made to sell, and they sold; and

his thousands of readers could as rationally charge their delight

in filth upon him, as a glutton can shift upon his cook the

responsibility of his beastly excess.

– Charles Dickens (1812-1870), *Martin Chuzzlewit* (1843-44), a novel notable for two of
Dickens's greatest villains; Seth Pecksniff and Jonas Chuzzlewit. The man in question
is Colonel Diver, representative of Dickens's satirical portrayal of America as a near
wilderness filled with deceptive and self-promoting hucksters.

You are aware that my plan in bringing up these girls is, not to accustom them to habits of luxury and indulgence, but to render them hardy, patient, self-denying. . . Oh, madam, when you put bread and cheese, instead of burnt porridge, into these children's mouths, you may indeed feed their vile bodies, but you little think how you starve their immortal souls!

– Charlotte Brontë (1816-1855), *Jane Eyre* (originally published under the pen name 'Currer Bell' in 1847). Here, Mr Brocklehurst discovers that Miss Temple has been offering meals of bread and cheese to her students – and consequently reprimands her with the words above.

He who distinguishes the true savour of his food can never be a glutton; he who does not cannot be otherwise.

– Henry David Thoreau (1817-1862), the leading American naturalist and transcendentalist, best known for his book *Walden* (1854), a reflection on simple living in natural surroundings.

'Come, come, Mr. Arabin, don't let love interfere with your appetite. It never does with mine. Give me half a glass more champagne and them go to the table.'

– Anthony Trollope (1815-1882), *Barchester Towers,* 'Chapter XXXVIII' (1857), the second novel in the *Chronicles of Barsetshire* series – satirising (among other things) the then raging antipathy in the Church of England between High Church and Evangelical adherents.

There lover-like with lips and limbs that meet

They lie, they pluck sweet fruit of life and eat;

But me the hot and hungry days devour,

And in my mouth no fruit of theirs is sweet.

No fruit of theirs, but fruit of my desire,

For her love's sake whose lips through mine respire;

Her eyelids on her eyes like flower on flower,

Mine eyelids on mine eyes like fire on fire.

– Algernon Charles Swinburne (1837-1909), 'Laus Veneris' (1866), where the speaker
repeatedly describes his empty, purely physical relationship in terms of bodily hunger,
depicting his love as 'a feverish famine in my veins.'

The other unpleasant incident, which for the first minute destroyed his good humour, though later he laughed at it a great deal, was to find that of all the provisions Kitty had provided in such abundance that one would have thought there was enough for a week, nothing was left. On his way back, tired and hungry from shooting, Levin had so distinct a vision of meat-pies that as he approached the hut he seemed to smell and taste them, as Laska had smelt the game, and he immediately told Philip to give him some. It appeared that there were no pies left, nor even any chicken.

'Well, this fellow's appetite!' said Stepan Arkadyevitch, laughing and pointing at Vassenka Veslovsky. 'I never suffer from loss of appetite, but he's really marvelous!...'

'Well, it can't be helped,' said Levin, looking gloomily at Veslovsky. 'Well, Philip, give me some beef, then.'

'The beef's been eaten, and the bones given to the dogs,' answered Philip.

Levin was so hurt that he said, in a tone of vexation, 'You might have left me something!' and he felt ready to cry.

'Then put away the game,' he said in a shaking voice to Philip, trying not to look at Vassenka, 'and cover them with some nettles. And you might at least ask for some milk for me.'

But when he had drunk some milk, he felt ashamed immediately at having shown his annoyance to a stranger, and he began to laugh at his hungry mortification.

– Leo Tolstoy (1828-1910), *Anna Karenina* (published in serial instalments from 1873-1877), described by Fyodor Dostoyevsky as a 'flawless work of art.'

'I've supped on potatoes and groats and am waiting to be sick. How about you?'

'I supped like the Lord in Heaven.'

'And what does the Lord in Heaven have for supper?'

'Nothing.'

– Jan Neruda (1834-1891), a Czech journalist, writer and poet – one of the most prominent representatives of Czech Realism. This quotation comes from *Prague Tales* (1878), a collection of wry, bitter-sweet stories of life among the inhabitants of the *Little Quarter* of nineteenth century Prague.

So long as you have food in
your mouth, you have solved all
your questions for the time being.

– Franz Kafka (1883-1924), *Investigations of a Dog* (1922); a story concerning the nature
and limits of knowledge – all told from the perspective of a dog.

So it's back once more, back up the slope.
Why do they always ruin my rope
with their cuts?
I felt so ready the other day,
Had a real foretaste of eternity
In my guts.

Spoonfeeding me yet another sip
from life's cup.
I don't want it, won't take any more of it.
Let me throw up.

Life is medium rare and good, I see,
And the world full of soup and bread,
But it won't pass into the blood for me,
Just goes to my head.

It makes me ill, though others it feeds;
Do see that I must deny it!
For a thousand years from now at least
I'm keeping a diet.

– Rainer Maria Rilke (1875-1926), a Bohemian-Austrian poet and novelist, described as
one of the most 'lyrically intense German-language poets' – renowned for his inherently
mystical writings.

FANTASTIC FEASTS VS. SIMPLE PLEASURES

Gently blow and stir the fire,
   Lay the mutton down to roast,
Dress it nicely I desire,
   In the dripping put a toast,
That I hunger may remove:
   Mutton is the meat I love.

On the dresser see it lie,
   Oh! the charming white and red!
Finer meat ne'er met my eye,

On the sweetest grass it fed:
Let the jack go swiftly round,
   Let me have it nicely browned.

On the table spread the cloth,
   Let the knives be sharp and clean:
Pickles get and salad both,
   Let them each be fresh and green:
With small beer, good ale, and wine,
   O ye gods! how I shall dine.

– Jonathan Swift (1667-1745), an Anglo-Irish author and poet, best remembered for his classic *Gulliver's Travels*. 'Cooking Poem: How I Shall Dine' (date unknown) – on the charms of simple mutton and good ale.

'Very astonishing indeed! strange thing!'
(Turning the Dumpling round, rejoined the King),
''Tis most extraordinary, then, all this is;
It beats Penetti's conjuring all to pieces;
Strange I should never of a Dumpling dream!
But, Goody, tell me where, where, where's the Seam?'
'Sire, there's no Seam,' quoth she; 'I never knew
That folks did Apple-Dumplings sew.'
'No!' cried the staring Monarch with a grin;
'How, how the devil got the Apple in?'

– Dr. John Wolcot (1738-1819), 'The Apple Dumplings and a King'. Wolcot was a
comical and biting English satirist who wrote under the pseudonym of 'Peter Pindar.'
The King in question is most likely George III.

To our great joy we discovered a comfortable room with drawn curtains and a most blazing fire. In half an hour they gave us a smoking supper and a bottle of mulled port (in which we drank your health) and then we retired to a couple of capital bedrooms in each of which was a rousing fire half way up the chimney... We have had for breakfast, toasts, cakes, a Yorkshire pie, a piece of beef about the size and much the shape of my portmanteau, tea, coffee, ham and eggs - and are now going to look about us.

– Charles Dickens (1812-1870), writing during a trip to Greta Bridge (County Durham), to his wife Catherine Dickens (1815-1879), on 1st February 1838.

Said Stiggins to his wife one day,
    'We've nothing left to eat;
if things go on this queer way,
    We shan't make both ends meet.'

The dame replied, in words discreet,
    'We're not so badly fed,
If we can make but one end meat,
    And make the other bread.'

– *Punch, Or The London Charivari*, Volume 1, 30th October, 1841 – 'Domestic Economy.' This poem comes from the very first edition of *Punch* magazine, a British weekly of humour and satire, established in 1841 by Henry Mayhew and Ebenezer Landells.

Not a deed would he do,
Not a word would he utter,
Till he's weighed its relation
To plain bread and butter.

– James Russell Lowell (1819-1891), an American Romantic poet. This verse comes from
the lengthy poem, 'A Fable for Critics' (1848) which Lowell prefaced with: 'I began it,
intending a Fable, a frail, slender thing, rhyme-ywinged, with a sting in its tail. But, by
addings and alterings not previously planned,–digressions chance-hatched, like birds'
eggs in the sand,–and dawdlings to suit every whimsy's demand, (always freeing the bird
which I held in my hand, for the two perched, perhaps out of reach, in the tree,)–it grew
by degrees to the size which you see.'

Now to the banquet we press;
Now for the eggs and the ham;
Now for the mustard and cress,
Now for the strawberry jam!

Now for the tea of our host,
Now for the rollicking bun,
Now for the muffin and toast,
And now for the gay Sally Lunn!

Now for the muffin and toast,
And now for the gay Sally Lunn!

The eggs and the ham, and the
strawberry jam!
The rollicking bun, and the gay Sally
Lunn!

The eggs and the ham, and the
strawberry jam!
The rollicking bun, and the gay Sally
Lunn!

The eggs and the ham, and the
strawberry jam!
The rollicking bun,
The rollicking bun, and the gay Sally
Lunn!
And the strawberry jam!
Jam, – Bun,
Jam, – Bun,
Oh, the strawberry, strawberry jam,
Bun ,– Jam,
Bun ,– Jam,
Oh, the rollicking, rollicking bun!

– William Schwenk Gilbert (1836-1911), *The Sorcerer* (1877) – a two act comic opera
with a libretto by W.S. Gilbert and music by Arthur Sullivan; the British duo's third
operatic collaboration.

There he got out the luncheon-basket and packed a simple meal, in which, remembering the stranger's origin and preferences, he took care to include a yard of long French bread, a sausage out of which the garlic sang, some cheese which lay down and cried, and a long-necked straw-covered flask wherein lay bottled sunshine shed and garnered on far Southern slopes. Thus laden, he returned with all speed, and blushed for pleasure at the old seaman's commendations of his taste and judgment, as together they unpacked the basket and laid out the contents on the grass by the roadside...

– Kenneth Grahame (1859-1932), *The Wind in the Willows,* 'Chapter IX: The Wayfarers All' (1908). The Water Rat packing lunch for the Sea Rat.

The cab pulled up before a particularly dreary and greasy beershop, into which Gregory rapidly conducted his companion. They seated themselves in a close and dim sort of bar-parlour, at a stained wooden table with one wooden leg. The room was so small and dark, that very little could be seen of the attendant who was summoned, beyond a vague and dark impression of something bulky and bearded.

'Will you take a little supper?' asked Gregory politely. 'The pate de foie gras is not good here, but I can recommend the game.'

Syme received the remark with stolidity, imagining it to be a joke. Accepting the vein of humour, he said, with a well-bred indifference—

'Oh, bring me some lobster mayonnaise.'

To his indescribable astonishment, the man only said 'Certainly, sir!' and went away apparently to get it.

'What will you drink?' resumed Gregory, with the same careless yet apologetic air. 'I shall only have a crepe de menthe myself; I have dined. But the champagne can really be trusted. Do let me start you with a half-bottle of Pommery at least?'

'Thank you!' said the motionless Syme. 'You are very good.'

His further attempts at conversation, somewhat disorganised in themselves, were cut short finally as by a thunderbolt by the actual appearance of the lobster. Syme tasted it, and found it particularly good. Then he suddenly began to eat with great rapidity and appetite.

'Excuse me if I enjoy myself rather obviously!' he said to Gregory, smiling. 'I don't often have the luck to have a dream like this. It is new to me for a nightmare to lead to a lobster. It is commonly the other way.'

'You are not asleep, I assure you,' said Gregory. 'You are, on the contrary, close to the most actual and rousing moment of your existence. Ah, here comes your champagne! I admit that there may be a slight disproportion, let us say, between the inner arrangements of this excellent hotel and its simple and unpretentious exterior. But that is all our modesty. We are the most modest men that ever lived on earth.'

'And who are we?' asked Syme, emptying his champagne glass.

'It is quite simple,' replied Gregory. 'We are the serious anarchists, in whom you do not believe.'

'Oh!' said Syme shortly. 'You do yourselves well in drinks.'

'Yes, we are serious about everything,' answered Gregory.

Then after a pause he added—

'If in a few moments this table begins to turn round a little, don't put it down to your inroads into the champagne. I don't wish you to do yourself an injustice.'

'Well, if I am not drunk, I am mad,' replied Syme with perfect calm; 'but I trust I can behave like a gentleman in either condition. May I smoke?'

'Certainly!' said Gregory, producing a cigar-case. 'Try one of mine.'

– G.K. Chesterton (1874-1936), an English writer, philosopher and journalist, often referred to as the 'prince of paradox.' This extract is taken from the metaphysical thriller, *The Man Who Was Thursday: A Nightmare* (1908), Chesterton's best known novel.

During the conversation several sea-maids came swimming into the room bearing trays of sea apples and other fruit, which they first offered to the queen, and then passed the refreshments around to the company assembled. Trot and Cap'n Bill each took some, and the little girl found the fruits delicious to eat, as they had a richer flavour than any that grew upon land. Queen Aquareine was much pleased when the old sailor asked for more, but Merla warned him dinner would soon be served and he must take care not to spoil his appetite for that meal [....] Trot wondered who would serve the meal, but her curiosity was soon satisfied when several large lobsters came sliding into the room backward, bearing in their claws trays loaded with food. Each of these lobsters had a golden band behind its neck to show it was the slave of the mermaids...

The queen's guests had no cause to complain of the dinner provided. First the lobsters served bowls of turtle soup, which proved hot and deliciously flavored. Then came salmon steaks fried in fish oil, with a fungus bread that tasted much like field mushrooms. Oysters, clams, soft-shell crabs and various preparations of seafoods followed. The salad was a delicate leaf from some seaweed that Trot thought was much nicer than lettuce. Several courses were served, and the lobsters changed the plates with each course, chattering and scolding as they worked, and as Trot said, 'doing everything backwards' in their nervous, fussy way.

– L. Frank Baum (1856-1919), *The Sea Fairies* (1911); a children's underwater fantasy
    novel, which has no relation to the 1830 poem of the same name by Alfred Lord
    Tennyson. Trot was a little girl who lived on the coast of southern California, whilst
        Cap'n Bill, her constant companion was a retired sailor with a wooden leg.

'O, Liz—you puffy Liz—

Get out of our way and mind your biz,'

cried the parrot.

'Creep-a-mousie, crawl-a-mousie, please move on!

We can't move a step till you are gone.'

'Don't disturb me,' said the lizard; 'I'm dreaming about parsnips. Did you ever taste a parsnip?'

'We're in a hurry, if it's the same to you, sir,' said Cap'n Bill, politely.

'Then climb over me—or go around—I don't care which,' murmured the lizard. 'When they're little, they're juicy; when they're big, there's more of 'em; but either way there's nothing so delicious as a parsnip. There are none here in the Fog Bank, so the best I can do is dream of them. Oh, parsnips—par-snips—p-a-r-snips!' He closed his eyes sleepily and resumed his dreams...

– L. Frank Baum (1856-1919), *Sky Island: Being the Further Adventures of Trot and Cap'n Bill after Their Visit to the Sea Fairies* (1912); as the title indicates, the sequel to *The Sea Fairies.*

He toasted his bacon on a fork and caught the drops of fat

on his bread; then he put the rasher on his thick slice of bread,

and cut off chunks with a clasp-knife, poured his tea into his

saucer, and was happy.

– D.H. Lawrence (1885-1930), *Sons and Lovers* (1913). While the novel initially incited a
lukewarm critical reception, along with allegations of obscenity, it is today regarded as a
masterpiece by many critics and is often regarded as Lawrence's finest achievement.

Though their life was modest, they believed in eating well; the best of everything: diamond-bone sirloins, three-shilling tea and the best bottled stout.

– James Joyce (1882-1941). *Dubliners,* 'The Dead' (1914). One of the longest of Joyce's *Dubliners* stories at just under 16,000 words, it is chiefly an extended reflection on the nature of life and death.

On those luminous mornings Adela returned from the market, like Pomona emerging from the flames of day, spilling from her basket the colourful beauty of the sun –the shiny pink cherries full of juice under their transparent skins, the mysterious apricots in whose golden pulp lay the core of long afternoons. And next to that pure poetry of fruit, she unloaded sides of meat with their keyboard of ribs swollen with energy and strength, and seaweeds of vegetables like dead octopuses and squids–the raw material of meals with a yet undefined taste, the vegetative and terrestrial ingredients of dinner, exuding a wild and rustic smell.

– Bruno Schulz (1892-1942), regarded as one of the great Polish-language prose stylists of the twentieth century. This scene comes from *The Street of Crocodiles* (1934), a collection of short stories which tell the story of a small merchant family from Galicia.

CULINARY
CALAMITIES

I seem to you cruel and too much addicted to gluttony,

when I beat my cook for sending up a bad dinner. If that

seems to you too trifling a cause, pray tell for what cause you

would have a cook flogged?

– Marcus Valerius Martialis (c. 38-104 CE), a Roman poet best known for his *Epigrams*;
a collection short witty poems satirising city life. Martial is widely considered to be the
creator of the modern epigram.

Old English

Now telle on, Roger; looke that it be good,
For many a pastee hastow laten blood,
And many a Jakke of Dovere hastow soold
That hath been twies hoot and twies coold.
 Of many a pilgrym hastow Cristes curs
For of thy percely yet they fare the wors,
That they han eten with thy stubbel goos,
For in thy shoppe is many a flye loos.

Modern English

Now tell on, Roger; look that it be good,
For of many a pastry hast thou drawn out the gravy,
And many a Jack of Dover (a kind of pie) hast thou sold
That has been twice hot and twice cold.
Of many a pilgrim hast thou Christ's curse,
For of thy parsley yet they fare the worse,
Which they have eaten with thy stubble-fed goose,
For in thy shop is many a fly loose.

– Geoffrey Chaucer (1343-1400), 'A Cook's Tale' from *The Canterbury Tales,* a collection
of over twenty stories written at the end of the fourteenth century; presented as part of a
story-telling contest by a group of pilgrims. The narrator is here speaking in jest, of the
Cook's questionable gastronomic talents.

A BACHELOR'S LIFE IS A FINE BREAKFAST, A FLAT LUNCH, AND A MISERABLE DINNER.

– Francis Bacon, 1st Viscount St. Alban (1561-1626), on the culinary perils of the single life.

O, he is as tedious

As a tired horse, a railing wife;

Worse than a smoky house: I had rather live

With cheese and garlic in a windmill, far,

Than feed on cates and have him talk to me

In any summer-house in Christendom.

– William Shakespeare (1564-1616), Hotspur speaking in *Henry IV,* Part I: Act 3,
scene 1 (1597).

Promises and pie-crusts are made to be broken.

– Jonathan Swift (1667-1745), 'Dialogue I' from *Polite Conversation* (1738), a book offering an ironic commentary on the banality of discussion among the upper classes of eighteenth century Britain.

I recollected the thoughtless saying of a great princess, who, on being informed that the country people had no bread, replied, 'Then let them eat pastry!'

– Jean Jacques Rousseau (1712-1778), 'Book VI' from the *Confessions* (1770). Although this famous culinary faux pas is commonly attributed to Marie-Antoinette, speaking of the French peasants (as 'Let them eat cake'), this book of Rousseau's *Confessions* was written around 1767 – three years before she arrived at Versailles from her native Austria.

At the inn where we stopped he was exceedingly dissatisfied with some roast mutton we had for dinner... He scolded the waiter, saying, 'It is as bad as bad can be: it is ill-fed, ill-killed, ill-kept, and ill-drest!'

– Samuel Johnson (1709-1784), the famed London diarist, as quoted in James Boswell's
Life of Samuel Johnson (1791).

As I looked along the yellow expanse out of which I remember its seeming to grow, like a black fungus, I saw speckled-legged spiders with blotchy bodies running home to it, and running out from it... 'I can't guess what it is, ma'am.' 'It's a great cake. A bride-cake. Mine!'

– Charles Dickens (1812-1870), *Great Expectations* (1861), Pip beholding Miss Havisham's mouldering wedding cake.

What a thing it was to see the potatoes bobbing about in the little pot; to peep at the squash getting soft so fast in the tiny steamer; to whisk open the oven door every five minutes to see how the pies got on, and at last when the coals were red and glowing, to put two real steaks on a finger-long gridiron and proudly turn them with a fork. The potatoes were done first, and no wonder, for they had boiled frantically all the while. The were pounded up with a little pestle, had much butter and no salt put in (cook forgot it in the excitement of the moment), then it was made into a mound in a gay red dish, smoothed over with a knife dipped in milk, and put in the oven to brown.

So absorbed in these last performances had Sally been, that she forgot her pastry till she opened the door to put in the potato, then a wail arose, for alas! alas! the little pies were burnt black!

'Oh, my pies! My darling pies! They are all spoilt!' cried poor Sally, wringing her dirty little hands as she surveyed the ruin of her work. The tart was especially pathetic, for the quirls and zigzags stuck up in all directions from the blackened jelly, like the walls and chimney of a house after a fire.

– Louisa May Alcott (1832-1888), *Little Men,* or *Life at Plumfield with Jo's Boys* (1871), the sequel to Alcott's celebrated *Little Women*.

It is a very poor consolation to be told that the man who has given one a bad dinner, or poor wine, is irreproachable in private life. Even the cardinal virtues cannot atone for half-cold entrees.

– Oscar Wilde (1854-1900), *The Picture of Dorian Gray* – first published as a serial story in the July 1890 issue of *Lippincott's Monthly Magazine*.

THE FRENCH COOK;
WE OPEN TINS.

– John Galsworthy (1867-1933), an English novelist and playwright noted for *The Forsyte Saga* (1906-1921).

Music with dinner is an insult to both the cook and the violinist.

– G.K. Chesterton (1874-1936), the 'prince of paradox.'

Mr. Leopold Bloom ate with relish the inner organs of beasts and fowls. He liked thick giblet soup, nutty gizzards, a stuffed roast heart, liverslices fried with crustcrumbs, fried hencods' roes. Most of all he liked grilled mutton kidneys which gave to his palate a fine tang of faintly scented urine.

– James Joyce (1882-1941), 'Chapter II' of *Ulysses* (1922), a landmark work of the twentieth century, in which the episodes of Homer's *Odyssey* are paralleled in an array of contrasting literary styles.

THE
CLASSICS...

As Ichabod jogged slowly on his way, his eye, ever open to every symptom of culinary abundance, ranged with delight over the treasures of jolly autumn. On all sides he beheld vast stores of apples, some hanging in oppressive opulence on the trees, some gathered into baskets and barrels for the market, others heaped up in rich piles for the cider press. Farther on he beheld great fields of Indian corn, with its golden ears peeping from hasty pudding; and the yellow pumpkins lying beneath them, turning up their fair round bellies to the sun, and giving ample prospects of the most luxurious of pies; and anon he passed the fragrant buckwheat fields, breathing the odor of the beehive, and as he beheld them, soft anticipations stole over his mind of dainty slapjacks, well buttered and garnished with honey or treacle, by the delicate little dimpled hand of Katrina Van Tassel.

– Washington Irving (1783-1859), *The Legend of Sleepy Hollow* (1820). Along with its companion piece *Rip Van Winkle,* 'Sleepy Hollow' is one of Irving's most anthologized, studied, and adapted stories. It follows a tradition of folk tales and poems involving a supernatural chase, including Robert Burns's 'Tam o' Shanter' (1790), and Bürger's *The Wild Huntsman* (1796).

Such a bustle ensued that you might have thought a goose the rarest of all birds; a feathered phenomenon, to which a black swan was a matter of course— and in truth it was something very like it in that house. Mrs. Cratchit made the gravy (ready beforehand in a little saucepan) hissing hot; Master Peter mashed the potatoes with incredible vigour; Miss Belinda sweetened up the apple-sauce; Martha dusted the hot plates; Bob took Tiny Tim beside him in a tiny corner at the table; the two young Cratchits set chairs for everybody, not forgetting themselves, and mounting guard upon their posts, crammed spoons into their mouths, lest they should shriek for goose before their turn came to be helped. At last the dishes were set on, and grace was said. It was succeeded by a breathless pause, as Mrs. Cratchit, looking slowly all along the carving-knife, prepared to plunge it in the breast; but when she did, and when the long expected gush of stuffing issued forth, one murmur of delight arose all round the board, and even Tiny Tim, excited by the two young Cratchits, beat on the table with the handle of his knife, and feebly cried Hurrah!

There never was such a goose. Bob said he didn't believe there ever was such a goose cooked. Its tenderness and flavour, size and cheapness, were the themes of universal admiration. Eked out by apple-sauce and mashed potatoes, it was a sufficient dinner for the whole family; indeed, as Mrs. Cratchit said with great delight (surveying one small atom of a bone upon the dish), they hadn't ate it all at last! Yet every one had had enough, and the youngest Cratchits in particular, were steeped in sage and onion to the eyebrows! But now, the plates being changed by Miss Belinda, Mrs. Cratchit left the room alone—too nervous to bear witnesses—to take the pudding up and bring it in. Suppose it should not be done enough! Suppose it should break in turning out! Suppose somebody should have got over the wall of the back-yard, and stolen it, while they were merry with the goose—a supposition at which the two young Cratchits became livid! All sorts of horrors were supposed.

Hallo! A great deal of steam! The pudding was out of the copper. A smell like a washing-day! That was the cloth. A smell like an eating-house and a pastrycook's next door to each other, with a laundress's next door to that! That was the pudding! In half a minute Mrs. Cratchit entered—flushed, but smiling proudly—with the pudding, like a speckled cannon-ball, so hard and firm, blazing in half of half-a-quartern of ignited brandy, and bedight with Christmas holly stuck into the top.

– Charles Dickens (1812-1870), *A Christmas Carol* (1843). *Christmas dinner with the Cratchits* is a classic scene credited with restoring the Christmas season as one of merriment and festivity in Britain and America after a period of sobriety and sombreness.

But when that smoking chowder came in, the mystery was delightfully explained. Oh, sweet friends! hearken to me. It was made of small juicy clams, scarcely bigger than hazel nuts, mixed with pounded ship biscuit, and salted pork cut up into little flakes; the whole enriched with butter, and plentifully seasoned with pepper and salt. Our appetites being sharpened by the frosty voyage, and in particular, Queequeg seeing his favourite fishing food before him, and the chowder being surpassingly excellent, we despatched it with great expedition: when leaning back a moment and bethinking me of Mrs. Hussey's clam and cod announcement, I thought I would try a little experiment. Stepping to the kitchen door, I uttered the word 'cod' with great emphasis, and resumed my seat. In a few moments the savoury steam came forth again, but with a different flavour, and in good time a fine cod- chowder was placed before us.

We resumed business; and while plying our spoons in the bowl, thinks I to myself, I wonder now if this here has any effect on the head? What's that stultifying saying about chowder-headed people? 'But look, Queequeg, ain't that a live eel in your bowl? Where's your harpoon?'

– Herman Melville (1819-1891), *Moby-Dick; or, The Whale,* 'Chapter XV: Chowder' (1851); a whole chapter in which the narrator, Ishmael, depicts the delights of chowder.

The table had been laid under the roof of the cartshed. Upon it there stood four sirloins, six dishes of hashed chicken, stewed veal, three legs of mutton and, in the centre, a comely roast sucking-pig flanked with four hogs-puddings garnished with sorrel. At each corner was a decanter filled with spirits. Sweet cider in bottles was fizzling out round the corks, and every glass had already been charged with wine to the brim. Yellow custard in great dishes, which would undulate at the slightest jog of the table, displayed on its smooth surface the initials of the wedded pair in arabesques of candied peel. They had had recourse to a confectioner at Yvetot for the tarts and the iced cakes. As he was just starting business in the district, he had given a special eye to things; and when the dessert was brought on, he himself, personally, carried in a set piece which drew cries of admiration from the assembled company. At the base of this erection was a rectangular piece of blue cardboard, representing a temple with porticoes, colonnades, and stucco statuettes all around in little niches embellished with gilt-paper stars. Above it, on the second storey, stood a castle-keep or donjon wrought in Savoy cake, surrounded with diminutive fortifications in angelica, almonds, raisins, and bits of orange; and finally, on the topmost level of all, which was nothing less than a verdant meadow where there were rocks with pools of jam and boats made out of nut-shells, was seen a little Cupid balancing himself on a chocolate swing, the posts of which were tipped with two real rosebuds.

– Gustave Flaubert (1821-1880); the wedding feast from *Madame Bovary* (1856) – the classic story of a doctor's wife, Emma Bovary, who has adulterous affairs and lives well beyond her means in order to escape the banalities and emptiness of provincial life.

All around them the cheeses were stinking. On the two shelves at the back of the stall were huge blocks of butter: Brittany butter overflowing its baskets; Normandy butter wrapped in cloth, looking like models of bellies on to which a sculptor had thrown some wet rags; other blocks, already cut into and looking like high rocks full of valleys and crevices. [...] But for the most part the cheeses stood in piles on the table. There, next to the one-pound packs of butter, a gigantic *cantal* was spread on leaves of white beet, as though split by blows from an axe; then came a golden Cheshire cheese, a *gruyère* like a wheel fallen from some barbarian chariot, some Dutch cheeses suggesting decapitated heads smeared in dried blood and as hard as skulls – which has earned them the name of 'death's heads'. A *parmesan* added its aromatic tang to the thick, dull smell of the others. [...] Then came the strong-smelling cheeses: the *mont-d'ors*, pale yellow, with a mild sugary smell; the *troyes*, very thick and bruised at the edges, much stronger, smelling like a damp cellar; the *camemberts*, suggesting high game; the *neufchâtels*, the *limbourgs*, the *marolles*, the *pont-l'évêques*, each adding its own shrill note in a phrase that was harsh to the point of nausea....

– Émile Zola (1850-1902), *The Belly of Paris* (1873); the third novel in Zola's twenty-volume series, *Les Rougon-Macquart*. It is set in *Les Halles*, the retail centre of a thriving food industry and landmark of Parisian modernity.

Instantly flinging a fresh cloth over the round table under the bronze chandelier, though it already had a table cloth on it, he pushed up velvet chairs, and came to a standstill before Stepan Arkadyevitch with a napkin and a bill of fare in his hands, awaiting his commands.

'If you prefer it, your excellency, a private room will be free directly; Prince Golistin with a lady. Fresh oysters have come in.'

'Ah! oysters.'

Stepan Arkadyevitch became thoughtful.

'How if we were to change our program, Levin?' he said, keeping his finger on the bill of fare. And his face expressed serious hesitation. 'Are the oysters good? Mind now.'

'They're Flensburg, your excellency. We've no Ostend.'

'Flensburg will do, but are they fresh?'

'Only arrived yesterday.'

'Well, then, how if we were to begin with oysters, and so change the whole program? Eh?'

'It's all the same to me. I should like cabbage soup and porridge better than anything; but of course there's nothing like that here.'

'*Porridge à la Russe,* your honor would like?' said the Tatar, bending down to Levin, like a nurse speaking to a child.

'No, joking apart, whatever you choose is sure to be good. I've been skating, and I'm hungry. And don't imagine,' he added, detecting a look of dissatisfaction on Oblonsky's face, 'that I shan't appreciate your choice. I am fond of good things.'

'I should hope so! After all, it's one of the pleasures of life,' said Stepan Arkadyevitch. 'Well, then, my friend, you give us two—or better say three—dozen oysters, clear soup with vegetables....'

'*Printanière,*' prompted the Tatar. But Stepan Arkadyevitch apparently did not care to allow him the satisfaction of giving the French names of the dishes.

'With vegetables in it, you know. Then turbot with thick sauce, then ... roast beef; and mind it's good. Yes, and capons, perhaps, and then sweets.'

– Leo Tolstoy (1828-1910), *Anna Karenina* (published in serial instalments from 1873-1877); an epicurean evocation of nineteenth century Russian high society.

Imagine a poor exile contemplating that inert thing; and imagine an angel suddenly sweeping down out of a better land and setting before him a mighty porterhouse steak an inch and a half thick, hot and sputtering from the griddle; dusted with fragrant pepper; enriched with little melting bits of butter of the most impeachable freshness and genuineness; the precious juices of the meat trickling out and joining the gravy, archipelagoed with mushrooms; a township or two of tender, yellowish fat gracing an out-lying district of this ample county of beefsteak; the long white bone which divides the sirloin from the tenderloin still in its place; and imagine that angel also adds a great cup of American home-made coffee, with a cream a-froth on top, some real butter, firm and yellow and fresh, some smoking hot-biscuits, a plate of hot buck-wheat cakes, with transparent syrup - could words describe the gratitude of this exile?

– Mark Twain (1835-1910), *A Tramp Abroad* 'Chapter XLIX' (1880), describing Twain's second tour of Europe. This longing passage comes after Twain's palpable dismay at 'European beefsteak'; 'they don't know how to cook it. Neither will they cut it right. It comes... in a bordering bed of grease soaked potatoes... a little overdone, is rather dry, it tastes pretty insipidly, it rouses no enthusiasm.'

Many years had elapsed during which nothing of Combray, save what was comprised in the theatre and the drama of my going to bed there, had any existence for me, when one day in winter, on my return home, my mother, seeing that I was cold, offered me some tea, a thing I did not ordinarily take. I declined at first, and then, for no particular reason, changed my mind. She sent for one of those squat, plump little cakes called 'petites madeleines,' which look as though they had been moulded in the fluted valve of a scallop shell. And soon, mechanically, dispirited after a dreary day with the prospect of a depressing morrow, I raised to my lips a spoonful of the tea in which I had soaked a morsel of the cake. No sooner had the warm liquid mixed with the crumbs touched my palate than a shudder ran through me and I stopped, intent upon the extraordinary thing that was happening to me. An exquisite pleasure had invaded my senses, something isolated, detached, with no suggestion of its origin. And at once the vicissitudes of life had become indifferent to me, its disasters innocuous, its brevity illusory - this new sensation having had on me the effect which love has of filling me with a precious essence; or rather this essence was not in me it *was* me. I had ceased now to feel mediocre, contingent, mortal. Whence could it have come to me, this all-powerful joy? I sensed that it was connected with the taste of the tea and the cake, but that it infinitely transcended those savours, could, no, indeed, be of the same nature. Whence did it come? What did it mean? How could I seize and apprehend it?

– Marcel Proust (1871-1922), *À La Recherche du Temps Perdu* ('In Search of Lost Time'), published in seven volumes between 1871-1922. Known for its theme of involuntary memory, 'the episode of the petites madeleines' has become one of the most famous literary scenes of all time.

...an exquisite scent of olives and oil and juice rose from the great brown dish as Marthe, with a little flourish, took the cover off. The cook had spent three days over that dish. And she must take great care, Mrs. Ramsay thought, diving into the soft mass, to choose a specially tender piece for William Bankes. And she peered into the dish, with its shiny walls and its confusion of savoury brown and yellow meats and its bay leaves and its wine . . . 'It is a triumph,' said Mr. Banks, laying his knife down for a moment. He had eaten attentively. It was rich; it was tender. It was perfectly cooked. How did she manage these things in the depths of the country? he asked her. She was a wonderful woman. All his love, all his reverence, had returned; and she knew it.

– Virginia Woolf (1882-1941), 'Boeuf au Daube' from, *To the Lighthouse* (1927); a landmark of high modernism which centres on the Ramsays and their visits to the Isle of Skye between 1910 and 1920.

Poetry makes nothing happen.

– W.H. Auden

The Writers On… Series hopes to show that words, crafted well, with thought, precision and imagination, can have a lasting impact on the world around us.

A good quotation can illuminate meaning, provide evidence or inspiration, pay homage or merely make the user seem well-read.

But what is the importance of being 'well-read'? Literature, although pleasing and entertaining in itself, is so much more than that. Like all the creative arts, it preserves ideals, and is often the last thing left to speak across the ages. It makes the otherwise non-existent, un-envisaged, and un-spoken widely available. As W.H. Auden so aptly states, 'Poetry makes nothing happen.' And this nothingness is exactly the point. With the act of reading, good writing makes the previously un-imagined, *possible.* Through poetry and prose, nothing becomes something.

Dealing with any aspect of our daily lives, from serious topics such as love and the environment, to sensual pleasures such as food, drink or sex – it is good to bear in mind those words which have peaked our awareness. With this collection of some of the greatest, *Writers On...* the reader will hopefully never be short of possibilities.

ALSO IN THE *WRITERS ON...* SERIES

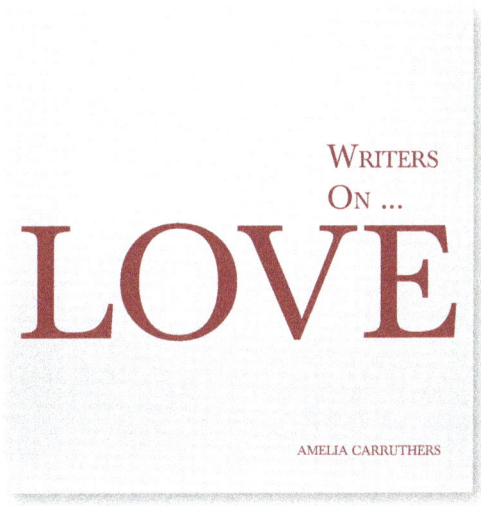

WRITERS ON ...
LOVE
AMELIA CARRUTHERS

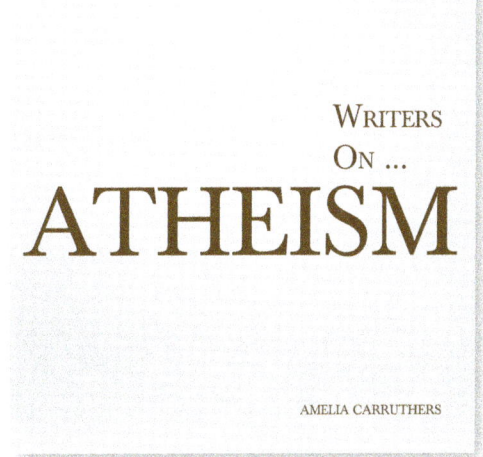

WRITERS ON ...
ATHEISM
AMELIA CARRUTHERS

WRITERS ON ...
NATURE
AMELIA CARRUTHERS

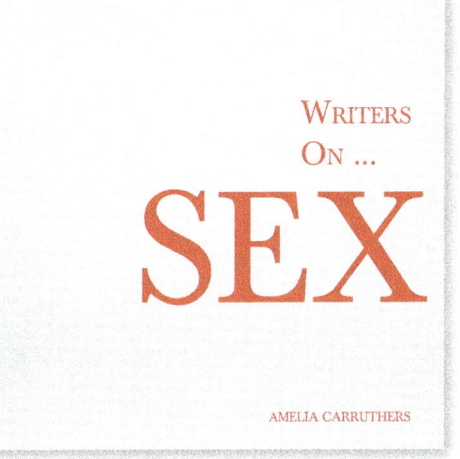

WRITERS ON ...
SEX
AMELIA CARRUTHERS

Lightning Source UK Ltd.
Milton Keynes UK
UKHW050629300322
400743UK00008B/139